I0453186

The Starting Point - Awareness & Hope (Self-Discovery)

Module 1/6 of Renewed Mind, Restored Life

A 6-Module, Self-Paced Coaching Course
for People Seeking Healing, Clarity and Purpose.

Dr. Josephine OlaTomi Soboyejo, Ph.D., CCLC

Published By

JOES Publications (Learnwithjoes LLC),

Marietta, GA, USA

All Rights Reserved.

No portion of this Document may be reproduced, stored
in a retrieval system, or transmitted in any form or by any
means, electronic, mechanical, photocopying, recording,
scanning, or otherwise, without the prior written permission
of Learnwithjoes LLC, Georgia, USA.

Contact: learnwithjoes@gmail.com

ISBN: 979-8-9943158-4-2

COURSE TITLE:

RENEWED MIND, RESTORED LIFE:

A Self-Coaching Journey to Healing and Wholeness
A 6-Module, Self-Paced Course for People Seeking Healing, Clarity, and Purpose.

Course Purpose:

To help Individuals renew their minds through Biblical truths, release emotional burdens through self-awareness and reflection, and rebuild their lives with confidence and faith-based strategies — without requiring a life coach..

Ideal For Individuals:

- Desiring Personal and Professional Development.
- Recovering from Loss or Grief.
- Recovering from Divorce or Separation from Life Partners.
- Seeking faith-centered Personal Growth & Transformation.
- Who desire coaching guidance but prefer self-coaching and moving at their own pace

Course Overview:

Format:

- Self-Paced Modules,
- Reflection Journal Prompts,
- Exercises and Assignments,
- Guided Prayers & Scripture Meditations,
- Printable Worksheets, and
- Affirmations.

Estimated Duration:

One module for 2-4 weeks or self-paced.

Module 1/6: The Starting Point — Awareness & Hope (Self-Discovery)

Theme: "Be Transformed by the Renewing of Your Mind." — Romans 12:2

Objective: Help you to recognize where you are, name what hurts, and believe that renewal is possible.

Components:

- Welcome Video: "You Are Not Broken — You Are Becoming." [YouTube Link]

- Workbook: reflection questions to identify emotional patterns.

- Exercises: The Emotional Awareness Wheel and The Emotional Inventory (What drains you? What strengthens you?)

- Guided Prayer: *Inviting God into Your Healing Journey.*

Module 2/6: Understanding the Mind–Heart Connection

Theme: "Guard your heart, for everything you do flows from it." — Proverbs 4:23

Objective: Discover how thoughts, emotions, and spiritual beliefs interact in your daily life.

Components:

Teaching Video: "When Thoughts Shape Your Reality." [YouTube Link]

Worksheet: *Identifying Limiting Beliefs & Replacing Them with Truth.*

Journal Prompt: "How does God see me today?"

Reflection Audio: *Meditation on God's Truths About You.*

Module 3/6: Healing from Within — Releasing Emotional Weights

Theme: "Cast all your cares on Him." — 1 Peter 5:7

Objective: Facilitate emotional release and forgiveness using faith-based reflection tools.

Components:

- Video: "Letting Go of the Past with Grace." [YouTube Link]

- Exercise: *Forgiveness Release Letter* (guided writing prompt).

- Worksheet: *Recognizing Emotional Triggers.*

- Prayer Reflection: "Lord, I Surrender What I Cannot Carry."

Module 4/6: Restoring Identity and Confidence

Theme: "You are God's masterpiece." — Ephesians 2:10

Objective: Help you rebuild self-worth and confidence through spiritual and personal affirmation.

Components:

- Video Lesson: "Rediscovering Who You Are in Christ." [YouTube Link]

- Worksheet: Your God-Given Strength Map.

- Affirmations of Identity and Confidence.

- Exercise: Designing My Confidence Action Plan.

Module 5/6: Creating Healthy Rhythms and Boundaries

Theme: "Let your 'Yes' be 'Yes' and your 'No,' 'No.'" — Matthew 5:37

Objective: Equip you to maintain peace and balance through boundaries, rest, and faith practices.

Components:

- Teaching Video: "Boundaries as Acts of Love." [YouTube Link]
- Worksheet: My Energy Map – Who and What Drains or Fills Me?
- Exercise: Design a Sabbath-Inspired Rest Routine.
- Prayer: Lord, Teach Me Balance.

Module 6/6: Living Renewed — Integration and Vision

Theme: "Write the vision and make it plain." — Habakkuk 2:2

Objective: Integrate insights into a clear, faith-filled life plan.

Components:

- Final Video: "Walking Forward in Freedom." [YouTube Link]
- Exercise: Your Renewed Life Vision Board (Printable Template).
- Journal: Commitment Letter to My Renewed Self.
- Closing Prayer and Blessing.
- Certificate of Completion (optional)

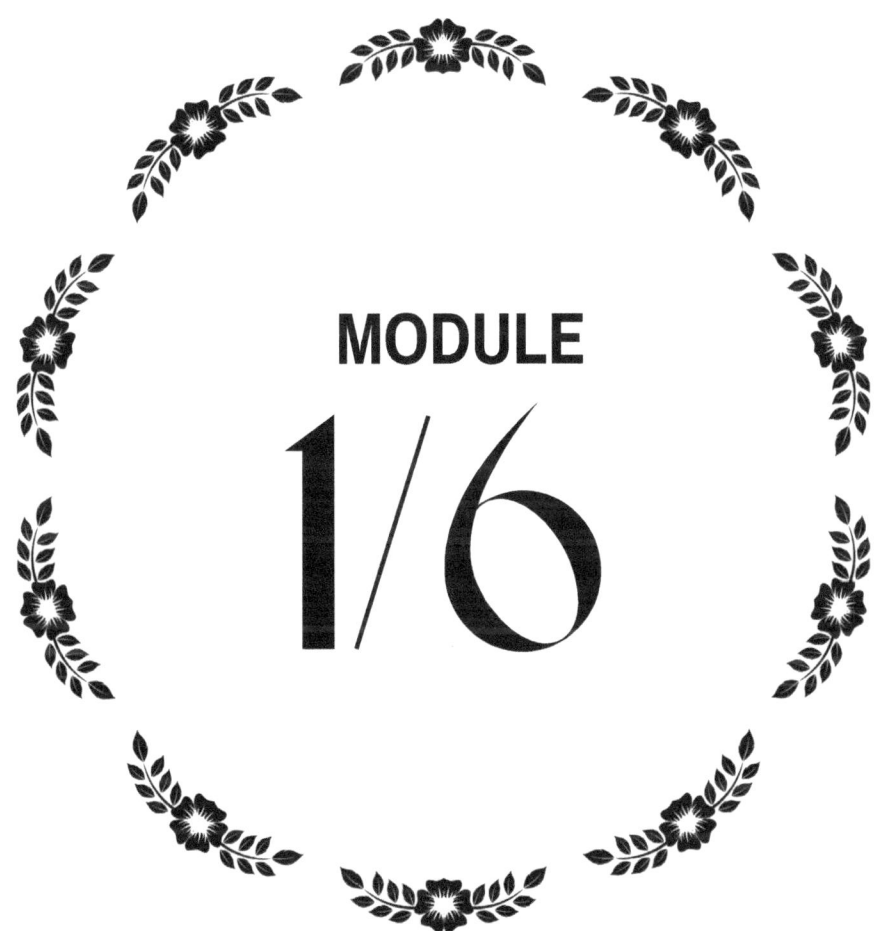

MODULE
1/6

The Starting Point — Awareness & Hope (Self-Discovery)

Isaiah 40:31, Romans 15:13, Jeremiah 29:11

─────── ★ ───────

Welcome to a Transformative Journey where new beginnings unfold with the Promise of each dawn. This module illuminates the essential foundations of Personal Growth through the powerful symbols of Awareness and Hope.

Table of Contents

The Coach/Author

Dr. Josephine OlaTomi Soboyejo, Ph.D., CCLC

———— ⋆ ★ ⋆ ————

Josephine Soboyejo is a Doctor of Philosophy in Philosophy of Religion & Theology, and a certified Christian Life and Health Coach with a heart for helping others experience renewal through faith, emotional healing, and purpose-driven living.

She is a Philosopher of Religion, a Theologian, a scholar, and published author with expertise in Ethics, Spiritual Formation, and Christian Education. Experienced graduate-level instructor, curriculum developer, conference presenter, and dissertation supervisor.

She brings a rich blend of academic excellence, professional expertise, and unwavering commitment to personal growth and transformation. Drawing on years of teaching, mentorship, supervising theses & dissertations of postgraduate students, and life coaching, she equips individuals to overcome inner barriers, rebuild confidence, enhance resilience, and live whole through the transforming power of God's Word (Wholistic Well-Being).
Her approach combines Biblical Wisdom, the Science of Well-Being, grounded in the principles of Positive Psychology, with reflective self-coaching tools and practical wellness principles, guiding each person toward a life rooted in peace, clarity, and courage. It incorporates evidence-based practices to enhance mental and emotional well-being.

"Healing begins when you invite God into your process. Transformation happens when you walk with Him in every step."

Dr. Josephine, as a Coach, helps clients align their goals with who they are, not what they do.

She is Certified as a Life Coach by the Board of Christian Life Coaching (BCLC), with additional certifications in Trauma-Informed Care Coaching and Mental Health Advocacy.

This multidisciplinary foundation enables her to approach the complexities of the human condition with insight, empathy, and a holistic perspective.

She is a Presidential Member of the American Association of Christian Counselors (AACC), a member of the International Christian Coaching Association, and a member of Biblical Counseling & Spiritual Formation Committee.

Establishing The Agreement

1. What would you like to Explore First?

2. In the Time you have, what would be most helpful for you!

3. What would you like to have by the end of this Module One?

4. How will you know you accomplished this?

5. Where are you beginning?

Differences between Coaching and other Support Professionals

--- ⋆ ★ ⋆ ---

Therapy: deals with healing pain, dysfunction, and conflict within an individual or in relationships. The focus here is on resolving difficulties arising from the past that hamper an individual›s emotional functioning in the present, improving overall psychological functioning, and dealing with the present in more emotionally healthy ways.

Coaching: supports personal and professional growth based on self-initiated change in pursuit of specific, actionable outcomes. Coaching is future-focused; the primary focus is on creating actionable strategies for achievin g specific goals in one's work or personal life. The emphases in a coaching relationship are action, accountability, and follow-through.

Consulting: approaches vary widely; the assumption is the consultant will diagnose problems and prescribe and, sometimes, implement solutions.

Coaching: the assumption is that individuals or teams can generate their solutions, with the coach supplying supportive, discovery-based approaches and frameworks.

Mentoring: A mentor is an expert who provides wisdom and guidance based on clients› experience. It may include advising, counseling, and coaching. The coaching process does not include advising or counseling and focuses instead on individuals› or groups› setting and reaching their objectives.

Training: the training programs are based on objectives the trainer or instructor sets. Though objectives are clarified in the coaching process, they are set by the individual or team being coached, with guidance provided by the coach.

Training assumes a linear learning path that coincides with an established curriculum. Coaching is more linear with a set curriculum.]

A Coach focus on Coaching the Person and not The Problem.

Welcome Video

"You Are Not Broken — You Are Becoming."

———— ⋆ ★ ⋆ ————

Watch on YouTube

https://youtu.be/DhcGRRVRdU8

Welcome to **Renewed Mind, Restored Life**: *A Self-Coaching Journey to Healing and Wholeness.*

This welcome video is your reminder that You Are Not Broken — You Are Becoming. Your story is not defined by your wounds, your past, or the moments that tried to silence you. You are in a process. You are being shaped. You are healing. You are rising.

In this journey, you will learn how to renew your mind, rebuild inner strength, reconnect with your identity, and walk boldly into a restored life of purpose.

This is not another motivational talk — it is a safe, faith-centered space where compassion meets transformation—a place where your heart can breathe again.

Whether you're stepping into emotional healing, spiritual growth, personal, or professional development, this program helps you move from survival to intentional becoming. You will gain the tools to understand your emotions, build resilience, shift limiting patterns, and align your life with God's truth and vision for you.

- You are not behind.

- You are not disqualified.

- You are not broken.

- You are becoming everything you were created to be.

Let this journey awaken hope, ignite clarity, and restore your sense of wholeness — one renewed thought at a time.

#YouAreNotBroken #YouAreBecoming
#RenewedMindRestoredLife #ChristianCoaching
#FaithBasedHealing #EmotionalHealing #WholenessJourney
#TraumaInformedFaith #HealingWithScripture
#ChristianGrowth

Self-Awareness

"Where Am I Now?"

★

PERSONAL DATA:

1. Name: _____

2. Birthdate: _____

3. Address:_____

4. Email Address: _____

5. Phone Number: _____

6. Occupation: _____

7. What do you most hope to accomplish with this coaching module?

   ➢ Provide specific examples or details about the changes you desire.

   _____

   _____

   _____

   _____

   _____

   _____

8. Describe what made you decide to pursue Self-Coaching:

   ➢ Explore your journey or any specific events that led you to seek Coaching.

   _____

   _____

   _____

   _____

   _____

9. Describe any previous experience with coaching:

   ➤ Include the nature of the coaching, what worked well, and areas where you felt it could have been more effective.

   _____

   _____

   _____

   _____

   _____

   _____

10. What do you imagine will happen if you progress toward your goals?

    ➤ Explore both tangible and emotional outcomes.

    _____

    _____

    _____

    _____

    _____

    _____

11. What do you imagine will happen if you do not work towards your goals?

   ➢ Consider the potential consequences and impact on various aspects of your life.

   _____

   _____

   _____

   _____

   _____

   _____

12. Who in your life is most supportive of your goals?

   ➢ Specify individuals and their role in supporting your journey.

   _____

   _____

   _____

   _____

   _____

   _____

   _____

13. Is there anyone whose opinion makes you feel scared, embarrassed, or unsure of pursuing your goals?

  ➤ Identify potential sources of external pressure or negativity.

_____

_____

_____

_____

_____

_____

14. What forms of Christian practice are comfortable for you? Prayer, Scriptures, Secular?

  ➤ Specify preferences and comfort levels regarding integrating Christian practices.

_____

_____

_____

_____

_____

15. Can you commit to finishing this Module? Are you willing to journal and take assessments?

   ➢ Clarify expectations and emphasize the importance of engagement.

   _____

   _____

   _____

   _____

   _____

   _____

16. Do you find that you act quickly once you have chosen a course of action, or do you take additional time to process/ contemplate?

   ➢ Explore your decision-making style and its impact on your ability to achieve goals.]

   _____

   _____

   _____

   _____

   _____

17. What has helped you reach goals in the past?

  ➤ Reflect on successful strategies or support systems.

_____

_____

_____

_____

_____

_____

_____

18. What do you consider to be your greatest strengths? How will these relate to reaching your goals?

  ➤ Connect your strengths to the specific goals you hope to achieve.

_____

_____

_____

_____

_____

_____

19. What would you like to change about yourself? How will this relate to reaching your goals?

   ➢ Identify personal development areas and link them to the broader goal-setting process.

_____

_____

_____

_____

_____

_____

20. Do you have other goals you have yet to mention because they are intimidating or feel too big to say out loud?

   ➢ Encourage openness about any hidden aspirations or fears.

_____

_____

_____

_____

_____

_____

21. Of the goals discussed, which do you feel is the most important for you to begin?

   ➤ Prioritize goals to guide the coaching process effectively.

_____

_____

_____

_____

_____

_____

_____

_____

_____

_____

_____

_____

_____

_____

SWOT ANALYSIS

1. What are your strengths?

_____

_____

_____

_____

_____

_____

_____

_____

_____

_____

_____

2. What are your weaknesses?

_____

_____

_____

_____

_____

_____

_____

3. What are you most passionate about?

_____

_____

_____

_____

_____

_____

_____

4.   What would your perfect life look like?

_____

_____

_____

_____

_____

_____

_____

5.   How would you describe yourself?
     ➢ Introvert (recharged by solitude)

     ➢ Extrovert (recharged by interacting with people)

6.   What stops you from having the life you want to have?

_____

_____

_____

_____

_____

_____

_____

LIFE BALANCE ASSESSMENT

Take a few minutes to think about your life and then rate yourself on the following scale with a score from 1 - 10, with 10 being completely satisfied and 1 indicating plenty of room for improvement.

1_____**5**_____**10**

- Physical Health _____

- Emotional Health _____

- Spiritual Health _____

- Family _____

- Finances_____

- Career _____

- Social Relationships _____

- Time & Schedule _____

- Learning/Growth _____

- Recreation/Fun _____

What would it look like for you to grow and 'flourish' – as God intends for you –in this season? (You can use the back or a separate sheet.)

Use the open space to share any additional information you find relevant.

_____

_____

_____

_____

_____

_____

_____

_____

_____

_____

_____

_____

_____

_____

WELL-BEING ASSESSMENT:

Please rate each statement on a scale of 1 to 10: One means strongly disagree or dissatisfied, and Ten means strongly agree or very satisfied. These Eighteen Assessment Points offer a holistic approach to help you gain deeper insights into all facets of your life and identify areas for growth and improvement.

Personal Growth:

A1.   I am satisfied with my current level of personal development.

A2.   I have clear goals and a plan to achieve them.

Relationships:

A3.   I am happy with the quality of my relationships with family and friends.

A4.   I feel connected and supported by my social network.

Health and Well-being:

A5.   I am satisfied with my physical health and fitness.

A6.   I effectively manage stress and maintain a healthy work-life balance.

Career and Professional Development:

A7.   I am satisfied with my current career path and professional achievements.

A8.   I feel motivated and engaged in my work.

Finances:

A9.   I am satisfied with my current financial situation.

A10.   I have a clear financial plan and am confident about my future.

Recreation and Leisure:

A11.　I make enough time for hobbies and activities that I enjoy.

A12.　I feel balanced between work and leisure activities.

Environment:

A13.　I am satisfied with my living environment (home, neighborhood, city).

A14.　My living environment supports my health and well-being.

Contribution and Impact:

A15.　I am making a positive contribution to society.

A16.　I am satisfied with my impact on others and my community.

Spirituality:

A17.　I feel connected to a higher purpose or meaning in life.

A18.　I regularly engage in practices that nurture my spiritual well-being.

PURPOSE & REFLECTION QUESTIONS

Purpose: To help you become conscious of your current reality, thoughts, and feelings.

Reflection Questions

1.　What is currently working well in your life, and what feels out of balance?

_____

_____

_____

_____

_____

_____

_____

2.   How do you usually respond when challenges arise?

_____

_____

_____

_____

_____

3.   What are the three emotions you experience most often
     these days?

_____

_____

_____

_____

_____

4. In what areas of your life do you feel most alive and fulfilled?

_____

_____

_____

_____

_____

_____

_____

5. When do you feel disconnected from yourself or from what truly matters?

_____

_____

_____

_____

_____

_____

_____

6. What recurring patterns or habits do you notice in your decisions or relationships?

_____

_____

_____

_____

7. What is one belief you hold about yourself that may be limiting your growth?

_____

_____

_____

_____

_____

8. Who are you becoming right now — and is that who you truly want to be?

_____

_____

_____

_____

_____

Unwavering Constancy

Sunrise arrives faithfully each morning, bringing warmth, light, and hope without fail. It's nature's most reliable promise of renewal and possibility.

Fresh Starts

Each dawn represents the precious chance to start anew, leaving behind yesterday's struggles and embracing today's opportunities with renewed perspective.

AWARENESS: THE FIRST STEP ON YOUR JOURNEY

Awareness is the greatest agent for change. When you see clearly, you can choose wisely.

Illuminating Reality

Awareness is like the first light breaking through darkness-gentle yet powerful. It reveals what's truly real, what's genuinely possible, and what deserves your attention and energy.

This foundational step transforms confusion into clarity, bringing hidden challenges and opportunities into focus. Without this essential awareness, hope cannot take root, flourish, or sustain meaningful growth.

Goal Reflections

Begin by revisiting your overall goals.
Reflect on your short-term and long-term objectives.

— ★ —

Goal Progress

1.   Short-Term Goals:

List your current short-term goals.

_____

_____

_____

_____

_____

_____

Progress made:

What steps did you take today to move closer to these goals?

_____

_____

_____

_____

_____

_____

_____

2.   Long-Term Goals:

List your overarching long-term goals.

_____

_____

_____

_____

_____

_____

_____

Progress made:

Reflect on the progress you've made toward your long-term goals.

_____

_____

_____

_____

_____

_____

_____

_____

_____

_____

_____

_____

_____

_____

_____

Hope

"What Do I Desire for My Future?"

--- ★ ---

PURPOSE & VISION-BUILDING QUESTIONS

Purpose

This section invites you to pause and reflect honestly on your current life state—emotionally, spiritually, mentally, and relationally.

The goal is to awaken awareness of patterns, perspectives, and priorities that influence daily choices. Through self-awareness, you can begin to recognize what is working, what is missing, and what God may be inviting you to change or grow in.

Key Aims:

- To gain a clear and compassionate understanding of your present situation.

- To identify emotional, mental, and spiritual patterns that shape your decisions.

- To reconnect with your core values and God-given identity.
- To lay the foundation for hope and intentional growth.

REFLECTION QUESTIONS

Use these questions as journaling prompts or guided reflection points. Answer honestly and without judging yourself.

Personal Awareness

1. How would I describe my life right now—in one or two honest sentences?

_____

_____

_____

_____

_____

_____

2. What emotions have been most present for me in this season?

_____

_____

_____

_____

_____

3. Where do I feel most alive or fulfilled?

_____

_____

_____

_____

_____

_____

4. Where do I feel most drained or stuck?

_____

_____

_____

_____

_____

_____

_____

_____

_____

5.   What areas of my life feel out of alignment with my values or faith?

_____

_____

_____

_____

_____

_____

Spiritual Awareness

6.   How is my relationship with God right now—distant, steady, uncertain, or deepening?

_____

_____

_____

_____

_____

_____

_____

7.   When do I feel closest to God?

_____

_____

_____

_____

_____

8.   What spiritual practices have I neglected or long to restore?

_____

_____

_____

_____

_____

9.   What might God be revealing to me about my current season?

_____

_____

_____

_____

_____

Relational Awareness

10. Who in my life supports and uplifts me?

_____

_____

_____

_____

_____

11. Who or what relationships bring stress or confusion?

_____

_____

_____

_____

_____

12. How well do I communicate my needs and boundaries with others?

_____

_____

_____

_____

Purpose & Direction

13. What dreams, goals, or callings have I placed on hold?

_____

_____

_____

_____

14. What is one area I sense God inviting me to grow or change in right now?

_____

_____

_____

_____

_____

15. If I could define one word for this season of my life, what would it be—and why?

_____

_____

_____

_____

Radiant Energy

Hope is the golden light that energises and motivates us forward. It provides the emotional fuel necessary to overcome obstacles and pursue our aspirations with determination.

Grounded Belief

True hope isn't naive optimism or wishful thinking. It's a grounded, realistic belief in potential - in your capacity to grow, adapt, and create meaningful change in your life.

Daily Renewal

Like sunrise itself, hope renews daily with remarkable resilience. Even after setbacks, disappointments, or difficult nights, hope returns with each new dawn, offering fresh possibility.

VISUALIZING YOUR PATH: THE SUNRISE METAPHOR IN COACHING

Standing at Dawn

Imagine yourself positioned at the threshold of a new day, ready to begin.

You're present, centred, and open to the transformative possibilities ahead.

Glowing Horizon

The horizon before you glow with opportunity and clarity. What was obscured in darkness now becomes visible, inviting exploration and purposeful action.

Illuminated Path

Your goals and challenges are now illuminated, no longer hidden in shadow. You can see the way forward with renewed perspective and confident direction.

Alignment and Goal Direction

"What Is My Next Step?"

* ★ *

PURPOSE & ACTION-ORIENTED QUESTIONS

Purpose Questions

(Clarifying motivation, meaning, and alignment)

1. What deeper purpose or value is guiding this next step in my life?

2. How does this goal align with my faith, values, and sense of calling?

3. What would success in this area look and feel like to me—internally and externally?

4. How does this direction contribute to who I am becoming, not just what I'm achieving?

5. What Scripture, promise, or truth strengthens my confidence to move forward?

6. Am I pursuing this goal from a place of peace or pressure?

7. How will I know this step is aligned with God's timing and direction?

Action-Oriented Questions

(Turning clarity into movement and measurable steps)

8. What is one small, practical step I can take this week toward my goal?

9. What support, resources, or accountability do I need to stay consistent?

10. What obstacles might arise—and how will I prepare to face them with resilience?

11. Who can I share my next step with for encouragement or prayer support?

12. What habits or routines can I begin that align with this new direction?

13. How will I measure progress and celebrate small wins along the way?

14. What do I need to release (fears, doubts, distractions) to move freely forward?

15. If I could take one bold action without fear of failure, what would it be?

16. What will I commit to doing in the next 24–48 hours to activate momentum?

MINDFULNESS EXERCISES

Engage in mindfulness practices to notice thoughts, feelings, and bodily sensations with clarity and compassion. These exercises build the muscle of present moment awareness.

Journaling Prompts

Use structured journaling prompts to reflect honestly on your current state and aspirations. Writing creates distance and perspective, revealing patterns previously unseen.

Guided Visualisation

Practice guided visualisation exercises, imagining yourself stepping confidently into your personal sunrise moment. This technique bridges awareness and action powerfully.

CULTIVATING HOPE THROUGH SMALL WINS

Celebrate Daily Progress

Recognise and celebrate daily progress as rays of sunlight growing progressively stronger. Each small victory builds momentum and reinforces positive patterns of growth.

Set Achievable Goals

Establish realistic, achievable goals that build momentum and genuine confidence. Success breeds success, creating an upward spiral of hope and accomplishment.

Share Transformation Stories

Exchange stories of transformation sparked by renewed hope. These narratives inspire, encourage, and demonstrate that meaningful change is truly possible for everyone.

INTEGRATING AWARENESS & HOPE: YOUR STARTING POINT

The Powerful Synergy

Awareness reveals the path with honest clarity, showing us where we truly stand and what genuinely matters. Hope light the way forward, providing the energy, courage, and motivation to take meaningful steps.

Together, these complementary forces create a powerful foundation for sustainable growth and transformation. This module equips you with practical tools to harness both awareness and hope for lasting, meaningful change in your life and coaching practice.

EMBRACE YOUR SUNRISE MOMENT

The darkest night is always followed by the brightest sunrise."

Daily Renewal

Every day offers a precious new beginning4your personal sunrise awaits with infinite possibility and promise.

Carry the Light

Carry this radiant light with you as you move forward courageously in your journey of growth and transformation.

Guiding Stars

Let awareness and hope be your constant guiding stars, illuminating every step of your path ahead.

Affirmation Set, Exercises & 30-Day Devotional

— ★ —

AFFIRMATION SET: RENEWED MIND, RESTORED LIFE

1. I am being renewed day by day.

2. God is healing my mind and heart.

3. Peace flows through me because God is near.

4. I release what no longer serves my future.

5. My thoughts are aligning with God's truth.

6. I walk in freedom and clarity.

7.   God's love anchors me.

8.   Hope is rising in me again.

9.   I am safe, seen, and supported by God.

10. Transformation is happening within me.

11. I choose grace over pressure.

12. I welcome God's peace into my day.

13. My emotions are valid, and God holds them.

14. I am growing stronger each day.

15. I trust God with my healing journey.

EXERCISE 1: THE EMOTIONAL AWARENESS WHEEL

This exercise gives you a structured way to assess your emotional state.

Instructions:

Rate each emotional state on a scale of 1–10:

Emotional Area	Rating (1–10)	Notes
Peace		Why this rating?
Stress		What is stressing me?
Hope		What strengthens hope?
Joy		What increases/blocks joy?
Fear		What am I afraid of?
Clarity		How clear is my mind?
Energy		What drains or fuels me?
Connection		Do I feel supported?

Purpose:

- Build emotional awareness
- Identify patterns and needs
- Begin renewing the mind through reflection

Journal Prompt

"What would it look like for me to feel renewed?"

Use guiding questions if needed:

- What would my thoughts sound like?
- What would my daily actions look like?
- How would my relationship with God feel?
- What burdens would be lifted?
- What new habits or mindsets would emerge?

EXERCISE 2: THE EMOTIONAL INVENTORY

What drains Me? What strengthens Me?

Purpose:

To help you identify emotional patterns, energy leaks, and life-giving sources so you can make intentional changes that support healing, clarity, and growth.

Part 1 — Emotional Drainers

These are people, places, habits, responsibilities, or internal patterns that pull energy away, leave you feeling depleted, or create emotional heaviness.

Guiding Prompts

Reflect and write:
1. Who or what consistently drains my emotional energy?

   ➤ (Examples: constant conflict, overcommitment, certain relationships, unrealistic expectations)

2. What activities leave me feeling empty or stressed afterward?

   ➤ (Work tasks, conversations, chores, environments)

3. What thoughts or beliefs drain me the most?

   ➤ (Self-criticism, fear of failure, comparison, perfectionism)

4. What daily patterns or routines create fatigue or overwhelm me?

   ➤ (Lack of rest, no boundaries, multitasking, procrastination)

5. Where do I consistently feel anxious, frustrated, or discouraged?

   ➤ (Specific environments or situations)

6.   What do I keep doing out of obligation instead of purpose?

Reflection Questions

- What do these drainers have in common?

- Are any of these drainers connected to old wounds or unprocessed emotions?

- Which drainers can I reduce, delegate, shift, or release?

Part 2 — Emotional Strengtheners

These are people, activities, habits, and environments that renew your strength, bring peace, spark hope, and give emotional life.

Guiding Prompts

Reflect and write:

1. What activities make me feel refreshed or energized?

   ➢ (Reading scripture, nature walks, journaling, worship, creative hobbies)

2. Who in my life fills me with encouragement, support, or joy?

3. What practices build my emotional resilience?

   ➢ (Prayer, boundaries, reflection, gratitude, exercise)

4. Which environments help me feel calm, safe, and grounded?

   ➢ (Quiet spaces, church, clean living space, nature)

5. What thoughts or truths strengthen me?

   ➢ (Affirmations, God's promises, reminders of identity and purpose)

6. What accomplishments or activities give me a sense of purpose?

Reflection Questions

- What do these strengtheners have in common?
- How can I intentionally add more of these into my daily or weekly rhythm?
- Which strengtheners do I need to reclaim or reintroduce?

Part 3 — The Emotional Map Summary

(Organize your findings into a simple two-column layout):

DRAINS ME	STRENGTHENS ME
People, tasks, thoughts, settings, habits	People, tasks, thoughts, settings, habits

Then ask:

- What patterns do I see in both lists?
- What small change can I make this week to protect my energy?
- What can I say "no" to?
- What can I say "yes" to that nourishes me?
- What boundary is God calling me to establish?
- What daily practice will help me walk in emotional strength?

Optional Spiritual Integration:

Scripture for Reflection: Nehemiah 8:10 — *"The joy of the Lord is my strength."*

- **Prayer Prompt:**

  "Lord, open my eyes to see what drains me, and give me wisdom to embrace what strengthens me."

- **Affirmation:**

  "I honor my emotional well-being as a gift from God."

Guided Prayer

"God, meet me at my starting point."

Father, You know exactly where I am today—every emotion, every burden, every hope. I invite You into this moment. Meet me at my starting point. Restore what is weary, renew what is broken, and breathe life into the places that feel empty. Align my heart with Your truth and steady my mind with Your peace. I trust You to lead me into healing and wholeness, one step at a time. Amen.

30-DAY DEVOTIONAL

Renewed Mind, Restored Life — A Daily Journey of Healing & Wholeness

Each day includes Scripture, Reflection, Renewal Action, Closing Prayer

Week One
DAY 1 — A New Beginning

Scripture: Romans 12:2

Reflection: Transformation starts with willingness.

Action: Write one area you want God to renew.

Prayer: "Lord, renew my mind today."

DAY 2 — God Sees Me

Scripture: Psalm 139:1–4

Reflection: You are fully known and deeply loved.

Action: Sit still for 3 minutes and breathe slowly.

Prayer: "Search my heart, God."

DAY 3 — Hope Rises

Scripture: Lamentations 3:22–23

Reflection: God's mercy resets your life every morning.

Action: Name one hope for this season.

Prayer: "Restore hope in me."

DAY 4 — Release the Weight

Scripture: Matthew 11:28

Reflection: God invites you to drop what's heavy.

Action: Write what you need to release.

Prayer: "I give You my burdens."

DAY 5 — Peace in the Mind

Scripture: Isaiah 26:3

Reflection: Peace comes from steady focus on God.

Action: Choose a peace phrase to repeat today.

Prayer: "Keep my mind stayed on You."

DAY 6 — Healing Takes Courage

Scripture: Joshua 1:9

Reflection: Healing requires brave honesty.

Action: Write one truth you're afraid to face.

Prayer: "Strengthen me for healing."

DAY 7 — God Is Near the Broken

Scripture: Psalm 34:18

Reflection: Brokenness does not disqualify you; it draws God near.

Action: Reflect on where you feel broken.

Prayer: "Be near to me."

WEEK 2 — Renewing the Mind

DAY 8 — The Power of Thoughts

Scripture: Philippians 4:8

Reflection: Your mind shapes your life.

Renewal Action: Identify one negative thought you want to replace.

Prayer: "Purify my thoughts."

DAY 9 — God Renews Strength

Scripture: Isaiah 40:31

Action: Rest for 10 minutes today.

Prayer: "Renew my strength."

DAY 10 — You Are Chosen

Scripture: Ephesians 1:4

Action: Write three things God says about you.

Prayer: "Help me see myself through Your eyes."

DAY 11 — From Fear to Faith

Scripture: 2 Timothy 1:7

Action: Replace one fear with a faith statement.

Prayer: "Give me a sound mind."

DAY 12 — Guarding Your Heart

Scripture: Proverbs 4:23

Action: Identify one boundary you need.

Prayer: "Guard my heart in wisdom."

DAY 13 — A Quiet Mind

Scripture: Psalm 46:10

Action: Be still for 5 minutes.

Prayer: "Speak into my stillness."

DAY 14 — You Are Being Renewed

Scripture: 2 Corinthians 4:16

Action: Write today's evidence of renewal.

Prayer: "Renew me day by day."

WEEK 3 — Emotional Healing

DAY 15 — God Heals the Heart

Scripture: Psalm 147:3

Action: Identify an emotion lingering beneath the surface.

Prayer: "Heal my inner wounds."

DAY 16 — Strength in Weakness

Scripture: 2 Corinthians 12:9

Action: Allow yourself to not be strong today.

Prayer: "Your grace is enough."

DAY 17 — Joy Returns

Scripture: Psalm 51:12

Action: List 3 things that bring joy.

Prayer: "Restore joy to me."

DAY 18 — Letting Go of Shame

Scripture: Romans 8:1

Action: Write what God has forgiven.

Prayer: "Free me from condemnation."

DAY 19 — God's Comfort

Scripture: 2 Corinthians 1:3-4

Action: Name one place you need comfort.

Prayer: "Be my Comforter."

DAY 20 — Courage to Feel

Scripture: Psalm 62:8

Action: Share your feelings with God truthfully.

Prayer: "I pour out my heart before You."

DAY 21 — God is Your Refuge

Scripture: Psalm 91:1–2

Action: Meditate on the word "refuge."

Prayer: "Hide me in Your shelter."

WEEK 4 — Wholeness & Transformation

DAY 22 — God Makes All Things New

Scripture: Revelation 21:5

Action: Identify one thing God is renewing.

Prayer: "Make me new."

DAY 23 — Walking in Freedom

Scripture: Galatians 5:1

Action: Declare one area of freedom.

Prayer: "Help me stand firm in freedom."

DAY 24 — Your Identity in Christ

Scripture: 1 Peter 2:9

Action: Write the identity God has given you.

Prayer: "Anchor me in who I am."

DAY 25 — Renewed Strength

Scripture: Philippians 4:13

Action: Speak strength over yourself.

Prayer: "I can do this in You."

DAY 26 — Mindset Shift

Scripture: Colossians 3:2

Action: Shift one thought upward.

Prayer: "Set my mind above."

DAY 27 — Gratitude Restores the Soul

Scripture: 1 Thessalonians 5:18

Action: List 5 things you're grateful for.

Prayer: "Give me a grateful heart."

DAY 28 — Transformation Continues

Scripture: 2 Corinthians 5:17

Action: Celebrate how God has changed you.

Prayer: "Thank You for transformation."

DAY 29 — God Is Faithful

Scripture: Deuteronomy 31:8

Action: Write the ways God has been faithful.

Prayer: "I trust Your faithfulness."

DAY 30 — A Renewed Life

Scripture: Psalm 23:3

Action: Write a commitment for your new season.

Prayer: "Lead me into wholeness."

www.ingramcontent.com/pod-product-compliance
Lightning Source LLC
Chambersburg PA
CBHW040904120626
46551CB00006B/642

* 9 7 9 8 9 9 4 3 1 5 8 4 2 *